MW00469314

SMALL ALTARS

Bronzeville Books, LLC
269 S. Beverly Drive, #202
Beverly Hills, CA 90212
www.bronzevillebooks.com

Copyright © 2021 Keli Stewart

Support copyright, support author's authentic works, and maintain a platform for the arts.

All rights reserved. No part of this publication may be reproduced, distributed, or transmitted in any form or by any means, including photocopying, recording, or other electronic or mechanical methods, without the prior written permission of the publisher, except in the case of brief quotations embodied in critical reviews and certain other noncommercial uses permitted by copyright law. For permission requests, write to the publisher at the address below.

This is a work of fiction. Names, characters, places, and incidents either are the product of the author's imagination or are used fictitiously, and any resemblance to actual persons, living or dead, businesses, companies, events, or locales is entirely coincidental.

Library of Congress Control Number: 2020951997

ISBN 978-1-952427-22-0 (hardcover)
ISBN 978-1-952427-23-7 (paperback)
ISBN 978-1-952427-24-4 (ebook)
ISBN 978-1-952427-25-1 (audio)

First Edition

10 9 8 7 6 5 4 3 2 1

Cover Painting: Ayanna Bassiouni
Book Design: Reggie Pulliam

SMALL ALTARS

Poems by
Keli Stewart

Keli Stewart

5/24/22

BRONZEVILLE™
— BOOKS —

Prior Publication

These poems have appeared in the following publications,
sometimes in different versions:

"after birth" (Gwendolyn Brooks award)
Quiddity

"venus"
Naugatuck River Review

"jumpinjumpoutjumpsidetosidejumponjumpinjumpout"
Calyx & *Meridians Journal*

"my mama cheating on my daddy with james brown"
On Becoming Anthology

"a way to get born"
Spaces Between Us Anthology

"revival"
Reverie

"there is something nasty i noticed about you while cyber-stalking your ex-girl-friend's photo album on facebook"
Muzzle Magazine

a poem for miss mary mack, coming down the street like janie crawford
Vinyl 5 A

"when a lover calls my body white"
The Little Patuxent Review Social Justice issue (Issue 11)

"How to Read Tea Leaves"
Rhino

"on turning 30"
Rhino

"But I say it's fine. Honest, I do.
And I'd like to be a bad woman, too.
And wear the brave stockings of night-
  black lace
And strut down the streets with paint on
  my face."

From "*a song in the front yard*" by Gwendolyn Brooks

Contents

II.
a way to get born

III.
porn star

IV.
how to catch a body

Self-Portrait with Spirit

I am afraid of loud sounds: my mother's body breaking down stairs, the treble
of swallowed tongue singing in her mouth, soup spoon like a wooden ship
cracking against teeth or grandmother dragged upstairs by her red ornery hair,
tasting teeth and blood. As a child, I find canines in corners with dead mice
and dream of them yo-yoing back into the mouths of wolves. I am afraid of teeth
and dream in gold fronts, mouth agape of rope chain and diamond. Mine, or
a body flung through glass-topped table with chrome base. The circular cipher,
them tumbling bodies look like a whirlwind of kin throwing fists.
I am afraid to see Black boys running, after rain when remnants of water
still come through trees and everything still but the corner camera's blue
flashing light.
I am terrified of water: viaduct floodings, car washes, popped
fire hydrants. I take baths on Sundays, the old woman of me musky
underneath weekday quilts. I test air for rain and direction, how I check
myself for ripeness. I am always ripe. I have at one point been called a fat ho.
I've had the electricity cut while the kids were in school twice. Had it back on
by the time they got home. Sold pussy. Sometimes I feel like a fat ho, my clit
like a lady cigarette between my fingers in dangerous places. I am afraid
of sleeping. My dreams wrecked by my mother's chaos or Freddy's
hand of blades. Guardian spirit, welding a machete, white dressed and
indigenous. Obatala or grandfather. Protector.

I.

we accept LINK

Small Altars

We don't begin in tandem, instead
it is I who stands back with painter's gaze,
surveying a windowed wall with
pleated duck curtains. kitchen grease
muddying each pane's sun or sky.
In this dream there is no window, only the wall
yellowed and indignant. A porcelain
Siamese cat grins from atop a shelf dusted in dirt.

My mother decides that this is the wall
that needs to be cleaned after your death
and begins hurriedly as if stricken
by thought: a clean wall. A balm.
She has bought yellow gloves and long push brooms,
the kind men in overalls use to white-wash
a city block after a killing, leaving nothing but slight trail
of dust and ornament. She has a paint bucket
full of Clorox and Joy. I smell its milky clean
foaming the rim before she dips the broom.
A taste like aluminum gathers inside my mouth
when I have to sit at her feet.

I know about the lingered packing of the dead.
Papa's good new church socks stored in drawers.
His pipe, with its rooted smoke mantle placed,
bottles he wrapped with rubber bands hold themselves
in small altars. All of his fury, not yet gone.
Even your dresser top, vials of perfume
dabbed on my neck. My small wrists
sit in waiting. Tell me, grandmother, how to be a woman.
I am underneath the kitchen table listening
to folktale and conjure, staring at the calves of hosed
women still unsure which part to shuck,
which part to save.

jumpinjumpoutjumpsidetosidejumponjumpinjumpout

when deedee jumps double-dutch
the whole ground shakes,
like she got bass in her feet
from a box chevy's trunk.
lean brown legs, scarless
and cocoa-buttered are pushed
into size 10's, pushed into white girls
worn down at the soles,
she got legs bowed like wishbones
centered 'tween the tight-white lips
of the double-dutchess' mouth,
fast talking liquor bottle glass
back and forth looks from people
who want this parking space.

when deedee jumps double-dutch
have to sing the whole song twice
like church choir,
cement curb lined with rolling eye
girls waiting for their turn,
four arms rotating in absolute circles
back and forth rocking,
jiggling mosquito bit breasts.
old women sitting lopsided on porches
gnaw dreams into gums,
wishing they could jump like that,
like deedee
who loosens fingerprints
and liquored breath,
all day saturday into midnight
when rope has turned to sky
and her feet, sore from
jumping into and out of have
begun to whisper sunday morning prayers,

after we stand in doorways
bellies full from dinner with
faces scrubbed clean,
still seeing the click-snap of
clothesline ropes near tops of trees,
deedee the double-dutch queen
traces circular outlines of
streetlight with her feet,
one in front of the other,
dragging her braided jump-rope
down the street
to get muddied in rainbow
oil puddles like our own
bare jumping feet.

wish-book

bel-air's came twenty a pack
boxes of blue tiffany in your palm
you unwound its golden zipper
as one undoes a plait.
my head, a turncoat of beads
not yet above bill's corner-store
counter, his dull nails,
round brown pennies
in my salty mouth
alchemists glass jars,
pickles and pig's feet

you kept shoeboxes of golden
tickets and easter clothes
and new white underwear dreamt,
wound tight with a junkie's rubber-band,
entombed top shelf inheritance,
my wish-book, my outhouse
catalogue, like coiled flypaper
color pages creased
as a playboy, hid like the
$100 bill in your hat box.

surely, it is you and i
in aretha franklin's pink cadillac
chiffon scarves tied at our necks
we drive to god-knows-where,
maybe it is Mississippi
we return, pockets bigger
than ditches, grandma's namesakes.

one summer, on the #53 bus
you swallowed your tongue
i watched it dance in your mouth
the moles on your cheeks flickered
and jumped,
all the coins became like teeth

in my mouth
metal in yours, a wooden
spoon scraping inside
of a pumpkin shell

all those wooden rhinestone
purses with hats to match.
we counted and recounted
wishes to infinity
as two factory girls in an endless
sweat-shop, depository
of girl dreams wishing
for every circled thing,
all the patent leather and silk gloves
kept in a box.

we accept LINK

when daddy leave we go to the welfare dentist that's what mama call it cause she don't like going but my tooth is swollen and mama say we don't have no money and that the lady she act like she doing you a favor by sticking her bony hand in your mouth even though somewhere down the line we paying her the door to the office act like it don't wanna let you in cause the carpet too high and the bottom of the door rub up against it and if you don't be careful you will push so hard you will fall in and inside there's all these people waiting to get they teeth looked at by the doctor who don't know nobody by they name and when it's cold outside it's cold inside and when it's hot outside it's hot inside and the woman at the counter she is brown with purple lips chewing gum all day and she got a LINK card in her pocket and i know it's that cause we got one too now that daddy gone so the lady at the counter don't say yes may i help you like the dentist we go to when daddy is home she
say
yeah
and don't look you in your face like ms. rosa does ms. rosa is the woman at the desk at daddy's dentist she is fat and good and if you have no cavities they take your picture and glue it to a big paper tooth and put it on a big board with the other kids with no cavities but the welfare dentist don't got one of them boards and she don't smile and she don't even close the door so everybody can know and see everything and while she is digging in your mouth all you hear is some baby crying.

Ode to a Black Satin Bonnet

Oh! Protectress of tresses, black satin
hotel for hair. Keeper of coiffed heads,
enclosed mushroom of overnight
pillow alchemy. You hair-setter!
You, fortified fortress.

Safe house of tendril and fibril
soldier of silk cap and quick weave.
Wind-buffer, pseudo-tam shapeshifting
on a black girl's head. Magician's white cloak
miracle of hair geometry and good sleep, guh

Tell-teller, griot of good hair, divine
prophetess of Holy Trinity: edges, kitchens, baby-hair.
Oracular roller-set orb. Sooth sayer. loc-layer,
bundle slayer. Lint's executioner!
How you anchor cornrows, spiral curls
and roller-sets. Night cap! Day cap!

Guh, you hat of hats!
Errand runner, report card pick-up
go-to, the sure-shot. You protective turban!
Not grandma's silk scarf slathered in brown gel,
Not the top of nude stockings clung as a cloche
fence around a Black girl's crown.

a black debutante at new awakenings home for pregnant girls

for our holiday service work
we went to a home
where pregnant girls
bathed their babies
in fifteen minute intervals
before an attendee checked
behind each ear

we smiled and politely nodded
and thought it was like the dorm
on *A Different World*

we checked our hair
in the hallway mirror
wrote notes and doodled
wild-eyed

we whispered between single rooms
where their ovular handwriting
drew curlicues with plump
hearts to dot every small "i"
on door tags like love-notes
and we nodded at the sweet smell
of cinnamon candles burning
and the garland trailing the threshold
mistletoe above playpens.

there were cookies on the table
a girl held a pillow to her chest
I'll Be Home for Christmas
played on the radio. We nodded,
unsure what we were saying yes to.

a poem for miss mary mack, coming down the street like janie crawford

we see your brown foot with bells
the heavy garter of melancholy
piquant behind your ears and underneath
the backwards black dress that catches us,
zig-zag ivy, buttons along spine rock
like the tasseled nipples of a pin-up.

it unnerves us, how our mothers speak
cautionary tales from front gates
we meet long enough to hush your
bare legs back into child's play chanting
morning after down to the house
where our mothers hang white sheets.

pink things

at ten years old, she goes to watch porn. tips downstairs where her uncles live, where red milk crates stand stacked by fours hold black tape with no boxes. only words. twat. cunt. ass. tits. words. she is careful with the door, plugged with a stained rag she puts back into place when she's done. in the same place where she found it, down there, that smells like old books, and rust and mold. one day she just pressed play. it was too hot out, her rope broke, her friends weren't home. she went down there. it was a thump, a sound like a heart 'tween her legs. thump-thump it went. thump-thump and kept going. she rewinds the tape and likes the woman's lips. they are red. they shine. she licks them and looks at the girl. the woman asks, "don't you want to feel like me? don't you want to do what i do. this feels good." yes. she rewinds the tape once more, back to the part where the woman screams like she's hurt. the girl knows that it doesn't, but maybe it does. it might. the man has his hand over her mouth. why is his hand there? the girl thinks. she must like his hand right there. maybe she does not. the woman's eyes roll back, her breasts move up and down, lines under where work was done are so clear and pink. he calls her a bitch. there is sweat on her forehead. she stands in front of the screen with her hand on stop. just in case some person walks in, she can find something pink to pick up and play with, a hula hoop, or some silly pink journal to write her silly thoughts and laugh and giggle and turn to nickelodeon. 4 and 5. 45. she has trained her fingers to know the buttons in the dark. with her pink polished nail on stop, she twists her hips. it makes the thump grow strong. her face gets so hot, she has to lie down on the couch to do it. a couch that smells like all those words, all those words kids say at school. her head is up, she looks at the door, the remote is in one hand, on the 4. she puts her right hand down there. the women are on their knees with their mouths opened for the man. to her, they look like two baby birds waiting for the worm the big bird has found and feeds to them. they share it, the two. they are not stingy. the women's mouths are open. they stir their tongues and grab their breasts and bounce up and down and make a noise in the back of their throats that sounds like their pink meat tongues will be swallowed soon. the man grabs his dick. he called it that, and tugs and pulls until he feeds them. they lick their lips. they lick their lips like he is so good. they stare at the girl. this feels good. the girl moves her body until the thump is a slow pulse, like bass from a car down the street that shakes the house, shakes her. then it leaves. slow, it leaves, she breathes and lies still, hand loose on the 4. she rewinds the tape to the beginning, turns it off, places the rag halfway in the doorjamb and runs up the stairs.

the couple next door

is fucking again
we hear them through walls
where mice copulate into infestation.
i press dirty glass to our beige divider
to twiddle thumbs & be them on the
other side during school days when our
children are gone & we are left to
stare at one another in post-partum
dullness while he grunts & she
screams & somebody gets their ass slapped
continuously & i can hear the sound
of bodies sweating & my mouth
fills with spit

i want to bake them a pie,
watch them eat as
muscles of their flesh move.
all i can do is snatch a glass
like a schoolbook spy
from our sink of dishes
in my girlishness
i am ready to make a noise
even if it wakes the baby.

venus

the fishnet cat-suit entraps like a poacher's vessel.
my body panics underneath, sea serpent in a crab net,

warped breasts, frantic during its snare and yank
a captive nipple, peeks cicero hoe, birth-pouch of fishwife

your hands intermittently haul fat between
my thighs, bucking tongue like schools of fish darting

three openings. the vixen red lipstick tastes like a good time.
i unhook my teeth, sambo mouth, warpaint and warm place

or bozo after drunkenness. so much webwork, i topple boats.
my one leg like botero's women, your dawdling hands

plankton small, fish and jetsam pour from rips as live-bait, mesh
of barnacles cling dowery. i'm sullied. honey-tongued.

below dam break, a sure-footed and porous woman,
a casting line stymied between your hands.

when a lover calls my body white

                                                        i am

aqua rocker and birthing stool fetish
blackamoor lamp and mccoy's mammy
muslin ragdolls and ivory heads

                                                        naked

ironcast pygmy, croquettes and quilts
cotton bulbs and blue shoes
mother of pearl pistol and snuffbox

                                                        against

bucket of knives and daguerreotypes
siamese porcelain and mason jars
a child's rocking horse and rice

                                                        blackened

secondhand pots and driftwood
cow-bell and carnelian necklace
bullet hole fedora and bag of hair,

                                                        skin.

bop: ramblin'

After Michael Afaa Weaver

you leave ill timed
like unwanted company.
when my menses won't arrive,
silent onlooker spinning gone as if
you have just witnessed a child
clapping or someone picking teeth.

i can feel the wind rising
leaves tremblin' on the tree

the bread end has
been eaten, car half-full
you left once while i balanced
mattress on my head, son
at my knee, went missing
on a motorcycle, thought
you died in a ditch.
for nine months i read the paper.

i can feel the wind rising
leaves tremblin' on the tree

when children call you father,
you hear a train coming.
ain't no bills due and it
ain't the first or the fifteenth
and we're in the middle.
i have tired and ran out of loving.

i can feel the wind rising
leaves tremblin' on the tree

Spring Haiku

Sometimes the niggas
who disappeared, pop back up
like perennials.

as you enter

you push into me.
joint like the breakaway
of a field-mouse burrowing
inside home. thrusts pat
sound from my belly.
bass rattles windows.

your body, a middle class
georgian in the suburbs
undaring, truth-be-told
ass, gilded brick-piece. hairless.
outside rain pokes like bees
thundering against cornerstone.

i think of all things. stroke
strumming itinerant woman
into home-place. your
sex like a would-be husband
of a woman who has yet to
know herself.

when you pull out,
long red drag marks
on white sheets.

II.

a way to get born

after birth

you drove placenta from amherst in a uhaul
thirty-footer flailing behind you, skidding ice like a tonka.

wrapped in paper, it somersaulted
cooler's plastic refuge, ice unfixing

biohazard symbol, lifeblood co-piloting.
you steered it home before unthaw, penniless,

on good faith and *i owe you* passed ticket-takers,
tolls and damages. this cargo, our freight

we wanted to migrate mississippi, fried chicken in shoeboxes,
boys in backseat catching monarchs and counting cows.

we wanted to plant it under an oak near hattiesburg, shaw, senatobia
my family tended and wailed rosehill's lone black cemetery.

i wanted to guide you to your kin. in my childhood, i got
stung by fire ants, walked barefoot down a mississippi road

named after big papa to the mailbox,
dusty country child, i grayed bathwater, slopped hogs

on his farm 'til skin blackened two whole shades,
gathered small pebbles in my palms to bless my city home.

we wanted a house the boys could grow in.
we wanted a yard wide enough to hold their black bodies

against metropolis and ghosts. we walked woodlawn
to hyde park window-shopping open curtains

like children playing that's my car through chainlink. we
wanted a system of belief. we wanted to pitch a tent on a cliff.

we wanted to see mountains and sweep
dirt smooth underneath a flat-back moon.

we wanted separate rooms, a blue house,
a little girl, then we did not.

i cleaned out our unlived-in apartment, not even mice remained.
stones heavy as babies heads lined windowsills.

a child's scribbled orange crayon, yogurt bursts like graffiti
on a blank wall. placenta in the freezer's nook.

yet, we said nothing. when we make love, we even say things
we don't mean.

come back.
come back.

a way to get born

grandma tied a towel around my belly, tight enough to girdle blackened
stomach. *breasts too, to get the milk out.* she folded me like a sheet
or a soldier's death flag. cotton. creases. kin. this is how she would
prepare my body. i'm a swaddled baby, a woman in a ghost sheet,
sexless, breasts collapsing underneath gauze, milk pushing through.
my soiled spots look like buttons of spray-paint. i want us touching.
i want him to feel his mama. when i hold him, he roots at my wish breasts.

on the border

at Superior and Austin Blvd.

farther down my tree-lined street, hemingway was born
the signpost reads with dovetails, garlanded oak door
farther down the other way, a boy is being mourned

where mothers snatch childrens' collars, cursing up a storm
i bolt three locks and tell my sons sleep closer to the floor
farther down my tree-lined street, hemingway was born

painted ladies are painted still, bikes deserted on lawns
cul-de-sacs and barricades and one-ways to *make sure*
farther down the other way, a boy is being mourned.

gunshots are firecrackers, blood street-swept at dawn
neighbors jog the morning jog, dirt dig minority poor
farther down my tree-lined street, hemingway was born

on this block, boys stand like trees, a gathered cypher of four
their black eyes and black skull coats romance the killing floor.
farther down their alleyway, their boy is being mourned.

on this block, dreadlocked black boys are herded, cuffed and warned
their black eyes and black skull coats romance the killing floor.
farther down my tree-lined street, hemingway was born
farther down the other way, a black boy, being mourned.

Escape Plan

in films, the mother-child duo
locked inside a starving hainted
house escapes, even after being possessed
and talking in demon-tongue or
even after the child has grown fangs,
almost devouring their mother,
or even after the child does go into the attic,
although warned, they run
from the burning flames together
hand in hand, front door a contortion of evil,
house collapsing behind them.

the child is usually
clever, like you. on screen, earlier
that day, we see a tween with headphones
rolling eyes continuously, at breakfast,
or folding clothes, at their little brother
or life. the father is…someplace else:
business trip, divorced or dead.
here begins the story of how a child,
sometimes a boy, grows into a man
over the course of an hour and 30 minutes.

there is always a leading moment
where the kid winces at the mother's escape plan
and grabs her torn and bloodied shirt.
the mother looks into the child's eyes
and the child looks into the mother's eyes
and says "Trust me mom" and they divert
the herd of zombies coming in the front door,

well, i am not that mother, but you
are that child. sometimes aloof in your own mind
as a bridge collapses.
last year, 36 chicago school children were murdered.
last night, i dreamt that your body was standing dead weight.
at 10, my thighs fall asleep while I hold you, big as a man
on my lap. in this dream, you would not budge.
insolent. scared. i could not get you moved from a crawl
space, no bigger than a crib.

in film, at the last minute, the mother-child duo
finds a secret serum to change the wolf back into a boy.
the furs folds into the skin, the claws retract
into the soft hands of a first-born. sometimes it is
the mother whose wisdom saves them both.
in real life, with your headphones, i wonder then
are you listening, when i am warning you to duck,
to follow your gut, to look both ways?

hopping fences in amherst, ma

this is a shortcut.
my son is seven,
already his head
hits my shoulder.
this is a shortcut
i say as i nudge
tip of my toe into
the honeycomb
metal of a gate.
a way to get to
some place quicker,

if you have to.

watch mama. he
looks like his
father who lives
in a world, but not,
a hero, he tells our
boy, he exits
and exists. exits
i am less heroic.
i make food. drive
to play dates. buy
underwear,
toys instead of bras.
my son tells me
that his father is
a m a z i n g. i think

of this with my
foot in the metal
circles of the gate,
while i teach him
to hop a fence as a
Black girl i never
had to hop. i
think this is
useful information.

that one day he
will be a man who
cannot outrun
life, but a short cut
is useful over an in-
the-way gate.

i want him to know
that you grab the top
like this. mama is
teaching him some
thing new. he has a
stick he has found
in his hand that he
picks up on these
journeys.

i straddle the gate.
shaking and wobbling,
teaching him to reach
the other side.

Meditation for Poor Mothers

Get you some weed from the boy
off Mayfield who favors your son.
Answer their questions with your field holler.
In your hand, it smells cosmic, like your womb.
The wolf smell of your second born,
feral, "outside" smell of germination.
You paid the water bill enough to keep it on.
Slather $15 EBT Coconut Oil on your untouched parts.
When the kids are grown, you will be supple
as Cicely Tyson. Somedays you feel like a pimp.
Sometimes a hoe, sometimes a goddess.
Sometimes you play songs for lost lovers
And have 1978 Eddie Levert thrust into
your shower bodyrolls. Sometimes you roll
yourself out unto the Soul Train dancefloor
Sometimes in the hot shower, you are the sea.
Sometimes you're the wave, sometimes you ride
wave. Until you leave the sea and you back
in your bathroom, the exhaust fan spinning your smoke
And realizing girl, sometimes you plant yourself
so deep, you must be a seed.

ana on the bus
Whidbey Island, Washington

you ride highway
like its four-legged
and smoking. mouth,
shotgun house straight
back to tongue.
the other black
woman in this
in-between town.

i have seen you
twice. once, the front
of an empty bus,
nestled you rosa
parks. purse
and shopping bag
on lap. abandoned
sister-seat. once at café
you cupped mug
coolly, its contents
malleable.

we quick smile.
although i'm touristy,
i wanna know
of hair grease and
smoked meat. like,
where you get it?
like, where it be at?
woods have dreadlocked
around my neck
dry hair, a hotmess.
the cut of yours, fresh.
as if you've accosted
hairstylist to cut around
your black-woman-thin-sides, with
shears.

we speak spacey. coded.
shonuff.
how you get here?
my sister.
where you from?
new york. you?
chicago.
product? oak harbor.
haircut? a white woman, did
a pretty good job too.
but first you ask me
of birkenstocks. thrift
store hand-me-downs
comfortable enough
to walk roads.

on turning 30

during my midday inadequacy,
i sit in my chair and look
at my hands & wonder if my hands
will beat my children & if my
children will flee from my house
& i wonder while my hands
are drowned in dishwater if i might
one day want a little bit of cocaine to calm me
& if i will ever need a bit of cocaine to calm me
between oprah & the price is right
& if my house will ever be clean &
if i will go to the basement to
clean up a lot & i wonder if i will
cuss

and lock my husband out for days
& beat my children & then forget
so that my mouth will forget sorry.
if I will hug them afterwards
so that my son becomes more
frightened of my touch than what
is in his closet & grows up to love
white women
& if they will call only on mother's
day & new year's because someone
told them to & if they will shroud
their mirrors in black cloth
before i am dead.

found money

the wallet smells of wintergreen.
slack in my palm, dollars curved
in small rolls. large bills. $20 goes
to the legless man who shows
me his toothless grin surely this
is a week's pay. the rosary amulets
are strung together like the braid
of the corner woman who sells
elotes and chicharrones. who would
own a pouch like this, an inferno
in my empty hands.

big mama at the marriott

for insurance casualties, they photograph
meat first. freezers hoard hamhocks
like tchotchkes or a black cemetery
ornament, housing image
of ground chuck, pre-slaughter.
wrapped in butcher's paper, foil
and plastic, its blood pools
in the third house
where papa pinned rosewood
paneling and dropped ceiling
like lover gifting a single corsage

bowlegs of a rusted nail bend.
roof falls into bathtub like
tattered toothpick hangs lower lip.
a leaf of cabbage, money blessing
nailed above doorframe like christmas
mistletoe, quarters in windowsill
throw salt and sweep dirt out back door.

she thinks of the hand-me-down
white couch, sooty footed children
dared not rest on its supple lap.
how she lamented the dirty sock
and sticky mouth.

how ordinary white
becomes when exposed to sky
and garbage bin, large enough
to hold a house,
all things immaculate and
piss-stained by rainwater,
like alley mattresses,
not by fire nor wreckages of smoke

smoke stays, water buckles and unglues
the shifting doorframe
innards scraped from within,
house bought blockbusting
from a little old Italian lady
who'd painted the living room red
and scratched its kitchen doors
until nails turned crowbar.

this is house that jack built
remember this house

in the first house, a Mississippi fire
raided pines victuals, ate cotton
quilts like scorched highway bleeds
the eyes. in a Cadillac, they returned
to find chimney haphazard,
backyard nesting clothesline
of what used to be a white room
meant only for entertaining
a room foreign to feet,
photographs left of hogs and horses.

My Grandfather Would Cry

Not when he could stand upright as a man
but after stroke, while sitting askew in the living room
hospital bed, tv placed before him like a plate. He hollered
at Tina Turner's legs and cat-called Vanna White,
yelling vowels, throat pregnant with spit.
sometimes she was a *dumb bitch* when slow to move.

You never knew how strong your grandmother was until
she lifted his body to sponge-bathe him and slide the blue liner
back underneath to catch his waste. Close up, the embrace
of lovers, or a child hugging a doll. She set him up
on the count of three. All the energy he had left going into that
pull and tug and sitting upright, right arm, a seatbelt heavy across his lap.

You remember when he went into his drawer and pulled
out a pistol. It was a mother of pearl 2 Shot,
the kind in cowboy movies your mother loves to watch.
The sheriff draws and shoots from the hip. That's how he looked,
Jheri-curl slicked back, horned amulet around his neck.
His wife took Big Bertha from her sleeping bed of knives.
You gonna shoot me motherfucker, shoot me! You were
watching cartoons. Many times, fingered the dust in between
the phone buttons, unsure who to call. You waited for the pop.
You think of this when you kiss him on the cheek, and he cries
sitting tall in the living-room, as a king.

what you come for

we, white smoke and naked
black kin alley cypher
rubbing palms, bonfire
of grade school pictures
wool red cross blankets
draped as navajo quilts
our children in underwear

we, warm eye of stove,
winter space-heater treaty
of open oven mouth and half
spent radiators sleeping
in socks with two blankets.
never warm enough.

our blue flies caught
inside plastic sheets hung
like curtains stapled to windows.
all slow dirges for roaches,
myth of picket fence.

> *won't you hide in this*
> *bomb-shelter with me?*

with the poems that burn
plastic bags full of elbows
and belly parts, sweet talons
and chopped white bone,
these pieces float like a factory
of burnt flesh, backwards
bar-smoke like pieces for packing
crumbled into black ash,
all the do-goody words
and incisors yet to cut

their spiral bound pre-baby of me.
what i remember of myself
singes like a choking noose.

                    what is left?

tuna cans and all the metal
that won't melt.

i want my body made of metal,
one of the things my drunk
cousin hammers every blackened
anything that sleeps for scrap.
from the back room
i hear his crashing.

i want some woman like me
to come along and toss me inside
a sooty burnt basket
wrangling
every remaining thing
that could have meant something,
even the scraps of quilt
and pictures of other families
fallen hard as a body through the floor.
fire shooting through
a bedroom window.

                    what was by that window?
                    what bleeds?

inside. shattered
bone-crack of my last good leg.

III.

porn star

porn star
*After "Keli's Home for Unwed Mothers"**

these breasts
belong to a woman,
pendulous, breasts like these
close to body,
hang while bending down,
flip-flop & sweat
yellow through a white bra.
have to gather t-shirt
in a knot underneath
for a break, tie it tight.

these breasts ain't good
for pinching while washing
dishes or finger play while
quiet in thought,
these breasts ain't good
for titty-fucking, porn
bouncing, thunderclaps or
smothering faces of lovers.
willy-nilly nor itty-bitty

these breasts, engorged,
you sucked milk from
like a snakebite. cupped
both hands over mounds when
we were too poor to pump,
spit the liquid in a dish,
it clanged metal like a bullet.

*film starring Keli Stewart, the alias of Black vintage porn star and centerfold Kim Watson.

42

Missionary Haiku

I like how you hold
my long titty in your hand,
outside, it's raining.

your new woman, outside your building when i drop the baby off

the dust is good for us. roof-men kiss bricks
with cutters, mechanical spurs scoring skin
of a corpse with day-marks. they're angelic
surgeons, housed within a serpentine
bittersweet. do you see how the dust falls
around us? do you see the rings left on shelves?
we catch it in our mouths as children throwing
handfuls of shadows over fences. our seesaw
pulley system. one yanks braided rope, while
the other ascends sounding bell.

but the dust, if we kick it, we make clouds
to disappear in. snow-tracks of my feet within
yours. we want to know where it comes from
before it was what it was. before it was shrapnel
in my eye. i like to 'in the beginning' it.
'me from your rib' it. bake it into a hard piece
of bread and break it as bird feed. two monk
parakeets shifting on a south-side roof. neon
blanket of green that began as two December
stragglers, lake michigan wind biting feverish plume.

the dust, it licks your forehead and you are golden
boy with golden child turning your back to the building, rising
to meet strangers who pass and outcry their palms
upward lifting you steadily, city night without howl.
the roof-men are tied triangularly
at the waist holding in what will not lift them
and here we are, in the dust, playing.

there is something nasty
i noticed about you while cyber-stalking
your ex-girlfriend on facebook

cock feathers flirt
early morning drip
and stutter. i mirror
cornfed thighs,
compare her
tinder. eyes like
a shih tzu's, weepy,
half-hidden
sturdy enough
to suggest she might
lick your leg upon arrival
or give you a good
fuck before dinner
for the hell of it and not
clamor at the thing
cold at her midnight back
and then again moving
toward mouth at 3am
where drool has pooled
since my childhood.

if she sees ghosts
and spits on sidewalks like
spittoon's chaw and kicks
panties to whereabouts
unknown like can-can
dancers throwback thigh
and ruffle. how i do. how do i?
gunmetal of my toe
like a sandal's sliver.
and if she wears a bra

and if you mind salt
and crumb. nipples peel
like an onion
areola black watermelon
seeds and i wonder if you might
want a summer's taste
and mumble seeds
in your mouth.
and if you eat the rind,

if she shaves
and buys elotes from
the greasy hand cart
i have learned to trust
how mangoes ripen
on his plastic shelf
and kiss slits of cucumber
outside the currency
exchange during cloudbursts
and folly.

and if she is a bad woman,
good girl or wild,
wolf i be.
if i should leave nappy
woolly or well enough alone
and have me stick 'tween
your teeth like corn,
your covetous mouth
like a guest who eats much,
then leaves.

three wing dinner blues

why you walking down the street with that greasy paper bag?
say, why you walking down the street with that greasy paper bag?
i'm bout to get you full off something i know you ain't never had.

you eating like you hungry and you sho' need a good meal
you eating like you hungry and you sho' need a good meal
if one woman won't and you a good man, hot damn! i might just will.

you eat the fat, the meat and the gristle too
you eat the fat, the meat and the gristle too
you a good three wing dinner cleaner, ain't gotta show you what to do.

come in offa that corner, come offa your corner tonight
come in offa that corner baby, come offa your corner tonight
i'm gone be your chicken bone, want you to suck me white.

you know i'm motherless, fatherless, sister and brotherless too
well i am motherless, fatherless, sister and brotherless too
but i ain't no wandering woman, don't fix no wandering man's food.
i said, i ain't no wandering woman, don't fix no wandering man's food.

prayer

jee-

       sus!
teach that girl
to be still.

old women whisper

i can't marry in white
maybe cream, its bastard
cousin, an idle pastel, silly
and fragrant as cold butter.

IV.

how to catch a body

How to Read Tea Leaves

I keep toilet-gazing into the tea leaves of a fetus divining bitter root, blood
flooding feet. All your pulpy tendrils spun into a dime, tiny and not-yet named
girl-child, shape-shifting in a small toilet cypher. I'm three months into this
love affair and throw myself downstairs twice. Once, mimicking a girlhood,
in a spinning house, the second, I ate pennyroyal and clover, trying to disappear
you into stardust and clay, hoping that you'd come back, in time.
Will you ever come back to me, now that I am my own bad mother and you,
a letting, your black eyes swirl in stool. I'm deciphering catastrophe.
My slow breath marked by yours.

A Poem for Dorothy

praise the bitch that got you
running into the cyclone
beyond fence, past the clothesline
that dried your ordinary things crisp,
the vast howling funnel and all
the freaks found jacking windedly
along the yellow road,
praise the ruby shoes
stolen from a dead woman's feet
you skipped shamelessly,
at midnight shimmying
atop her ash, eyes toward home,
they smelled of smoke

praise the checkered dress
skin within skin, the poppies,
red as dusk, and hot night.
five and dime socks
pigtails and striped stockings
and the men hammering
a make-shift gate.

praise the shut door and raised house
and all the broken glass spinning
in the whirlwind with you,
cheeks sliced with warrior marks,
like a girl from the Ickes.
praise cotton quilts, brown and folded
that rose to meet your tears like the dead.

my mama cheating on my daddy with james brown

i ain't playing. ever since i was me,
they be in the kitchen making music with the dish-soap.

she wear hot pants mumbling over grits,
smacking baby roaches flat against walls, bringing fingers down in a snap.

she be snaking and grinding over grease spots.
they keep door closed. i can't see, but i hear.

he be talking 'bout *please, please*
please, please, please,
please   she be saying   *give it to me james*   *do it james*   *sing it*
james

after a while smells come from the kitchen. they sex smoke smell like steak.
washing powder. on thursdays always chicken.

other times it smell like some woman's tears.
james brown be with her over the sink where sometime she just stare
dishwater.

my daddy work nights, sleep days.

that's how james brown started giving her something good. she say they be
doing something musical, not sexual.

i don't know how she do it. cook and cheat at the same time. wash and cheat.
iron and cheat. fold and cheat. mop and cheat. sing and cheat.

i don't know how she do it. housewife at 25. one child, three children
dead, manage two men.

who could love a writer?

who knows how to love someone
who sees no Sunday in Sunday
dinner and spits in the pots?
someone who burns pots
and lets them soak for seven
days and on the seventh day,
she rested.

someone as subversive as this
surely does not love the baby jesus
and is not a saint. who will love
this shepherded woman in her woolly
coat with her woolly hair calling
sinners in?

who would love someone as ugly?
her mother's fists remind her
of a dick. who could love
someone who compares her
mother's fist to a dick?

who could say dick?
who
has been raped?

who could love a rain dancer
calling the storm on like a
child cries to a swollen mother
praying for cloud break. who
would love this sky watcher
this teller of days, this shade-shutter?

who will love the ink?
the triggering finger, the trigger
finger. who ropes the crying
woman to train-track
and waits?

Love Poem #3

Since I've been in love, I'm so sappy. My friends have problems, I don't.
I am a flower vase, blooming beside myself. All the images of soil between
fingers of farmers, I am that soil caught in fingernail. Black. Stubborn
and you, that farmer. Tilling. The gas got cut off but we lie in a bed so warm, we
undress in our sleep. Teasing with titty and tongue. I look at you like
what you want from me? Piss-colored Black girl, talking to ghosts, blazing
weed at 2am staring at you. Big bellied and crass, refined in make believe.
Somebody told me I am no one's wife, yet here you have chosen me.

women's work kwansaba

For Dinky West and Barbara Partee Jones

I.

grandma washed with knife 'tween the whites,
cutting easily into cotton blends on washday
big bertha jabbed polite linen was good
for cutting sundry meats, sliced bloody loin
into dapper slits and paused swinging fists
'lowed a cooing baby to be rocked
to nursing noon day sleep in peace.

II.

this picture when we first got married
photo man looked too many damn times.
captured me, hammer to my naked head,
i know the meaning of the threshing floor
stone and pillars, a quiet man heaving,
against woman under him, woman in garden,
woman on her knees in streets, praying.

III.

i'm jook that made the joint bad
a mean mug hitter, a pageant switchblade,
widdled by a woman who needs knife
she courts my handle sweet at midnight
queen of wands, kitchen heavy nigger beater
i, upright in my bed of beds
standing, like i got two man legs.

IV.

this here a fine knife. ain't untaught,
don't muddle or mince, straight, no chaser
skilled in my hand, roguish alley dagger
undo thread and vestiges, strong, an ax.
bet i could cut down a tree
who named me this silly name, dinky?
small, trifling, wrong name for a woman.

on turning 40

A black girl's body can float. Not Tallahatchie or missing, but once, in my childhood bedroom all the happy/sad of me balanced two magician's fingertips and rose. Spirit-body stopping. Only when my nose touched ceiling, not ready yet for death. I could have kept going. *Fine with me.* In that house, where one day, I would be bound to that room. Mother in the closet kicking high-heeled shoes into hallway. Mother unplugging all the phones. The speaker box of her mind on bass. My body in the baseline. Her fists the beat, beating.

I think myself into that room now, floating in its granular air. Blue fuzz on my face, *I Love Lucy* at midnight. Tongue forever seized with stutter since. Implants in my palms left scar marks, a chorus of ghosts in my eardrum singing bedside. Mouth slack. Mouth loveless, the downward turn, the Westside machisma, the two-headedness. I think of myself as floating and only now return to see the body I floated from. I expect casket, suited body ready to be called home, a ragged lip line, dead-girl ponytail, and not a slumbering child, curled in that room in a corner, so small, I almost missed her. So small, I forgot about the myth of abduction, the tales I made to survive. I remember now leaving that form. It taught me that spirit would survive a body.

Letters for Strangers

I leave all mail inside the mailbox, a months' worth of bills,
letters for strangers, birthday wishes, even a card from an ex,
I opened and shoved back inside its thin paper.
That was the first time I saw his left-handed penmanship,
ring finger still wrapped in metal oddly holding an ordinary Bic.
Inside: a sentence and signature. His fingers still smelled like me,
like the fingers of the boy who molded my body on back
of school buses in 4th grade. So tall over schoolteachers, I remember
him hawked atop a washroom stall staring. The crotch of my panties
just starting to leak yellow sunlight. For my birthday, a card with a cat
on the cover *You're So Special to Me*. How he scribbled the "B" was reckless.
Like a man hell-bent on leaping from dark places and asking *do you feel safe?*
Like a boy, who liked a girl and didn't know how
        to show her.

You: Glad to Hear
3:49 AM

Let's pretend you walked me to my car
and seen the side by side paw tracks of two alley cats
like a herd of beasts in the pre-dawn slush
two by two, their feral bodies shouldering one another
down a city block

Outside your fence, you could have slipped, as I did.
Our bodies falling flagrantly as they once had.
You could have caught me underneath corner's blue flashing light
and maybe for a second seen the stardust of my eyes
and maybe for a second seen how dwarf rose bushes
still bloom curbside, red in the frost.

You would have chosen one and felt my heart's bass beating
through a wool winter's coat, body blushing underneath.
You were supposed to have opened my door.
The quickening snowfall settling tongues as our mouths met.
You would have stood front porch, unbent by the cold,
a stray cat weaving your legs until I warmed.

Inside my car, I see your bedroom's dim light go black
the last remaining light emptying in this first snow.
All the windows of your old house curtainless, like mine
the bastard feeling of each bare room.

Dear Tinder Lover from Portland

Since we last talked, the doorknob you fixed crumbled inside
my handshake and weeds whacked came back sprouting
poison hemlock along wooden gate. I am now the witch
in the big house, how overgrown bushes mimic my belly.
I walk outdoors barefoot, picking up Patron bottles, front yard
offerings at daybreak, hair a wooded crown of sumac,
blue dye like face paint, eyes no longer burning from second sight.
I am not the empty-eyed woman you assumed me to be.
On blessed days, I wear white, holy-ghosting this lean-to house
with sage and praise dance. I leave tobacco leaves, whiskey, oranges for
my grandmothers who possess me over pots and wake me from child-dreams
as books fall from dusty shelves. You mistook dust for laziness
not sediment from frankincense as house blessing, cayenne for trespassers.
A crown of orbs floats in a century-old house. You taught me in your silence
how to talk to the dead. I dream of a green-eyed wolf
stalking the outposts of my front porch, paw over paw, furred back scraping
wooden beams. With flowers, you are outside my front gate's good spell.
What's keeping this house standing is holy water.

revival

"If we're gonna be buddies, you better bone up on the rules."
                    Evillene "*The Wiz*"

be a bird of paradise
hustle your fine
male plumage,
make feathers a potent
jook decanter,
act against machismo,
cool pose and heartbreak
sooner or later
bend your knee-caps
showstopper,
hop on one leg
give me something to
write home about,
make me leave
my mama's house,
be a ghetto christmas
pageant, procreation
alone is easy.
crowd please me
be a sword-swallower,
act a damn fool

unlock lion's cage
stick your head in,
lemme hear your
high-note
give me slickest
swagger
make me a bad woman,
i want what you got,
get me where you at,
make me your tent-revival
give me your Holy Ghost hour,
be sunday spectacle
write your decalogue
make your banner spangled
puff them feathers baby
less you be slaughtered
by another.

Self-portrait: Me with Hair Like Frederick Douglass

This is me with a winded woolly
afro. This is me with red lipstick.
This is me with denim pants and
camel toe. This is me, barefoot.
This is me hopping a gate. This
is me in white lace mopping (moping).
This is me in a flop house, I mean
trap house   holding a sunflower.

Acknowledgements

Many thanks to the Gwendolyn Brooks Center for Black Literature and Creative Writing, Hedgebrook, the Illinois Center for the Book and Augusta Savage Gallery. I am eternally grateful to my classmates and professors at Chicago State University; Haki Madhubuti, Quraysh Ali Lansana, and Kelly Norman Ellis, and also to Sheila Baldwin, Cadence Wynters, Paul Carter Harrison, and Rose Blouin from Columbia College. The Women of Color Leadership Network and The Department of Afro-American Studies at the University of Massachusetts-Amherst who offered me new language. So much appreciation for Tyehimba Jess, Sonia Sanchez, Millicent Jackson, Eraina Ferguson, Jennifer Steele, LeTrice Buckingham, Krista Franklin, Roger Bonair-Agard and to FreeStreet Theater, who taught me how to breathe, Woman Made Gallery, my VONA and Callaloo kin and my real blood. Lastly, a huge hug of gratitude to my sons.

CPSIA information can be obtained
at www.ICGtesting.com
Printed in the USA
LVHW020753100422
715552LV00007B/119